Tiger Tales 2

PUPIL'S BOOK

My name is _____.

How are you, Tiger?	page	3
1 A Surprise	page	7
2 A New Pet	page	17
Tiger Review 1	page	27
3 Where's my coat?	page	29
4 Break Time	page	39
Tiger Review 2	page	49
5 What's the matter?	page	51
6 On Holiday	page	61
Tiger Review 3	page	71
Halloween	page	74
Christmas	page	76
Carnival	page	78
Picture Dictionary	page	80
Cut-outs	page	83
Syllabus	page	96

Carol Read • Mark Ormerod

MACMILLAN

Macmillan Education
4 Crinan Street
London N1 9XW
A division of Springer Nature Limited
Companies and representatives throughout the world

ISBN 978 0 230 43088 4

Text © Carol Read and Mark Ormerod 2013
Design and illustration © Springer Nature Limited 2013
First published 2013
All rights reserved; no part of this publication may be reproduced, stored in a retrieval system, transmitted in any form, or by any means, electronic, mechanical, photocopying, recording, or otherwise, without the prior written permission of the publishers.
Designed by Blooberry Design Ltd
Illustrated by Rodrigo Folguiera, Kelly Kennedy, Jan McCafferty, Andy Parker, Anthony Rule and Jo Taylor
Cover design by Astwood Design Consultancy
Cover illustration by Rodrigo Folgueira
Cover photographs provided by Corbis; Getty; Macmillan Publishers Ltd/ Stuart Cox; Photodisc; Stockbyte
Songs produced and arranged by Tom, Dick and Debbie Productions
Recordings produced and arranged by RBA Productions
Pictures researched by Victoria Gaunt

Authors' acknowledgments
We would like to thank everyone at Macmillan Education in the UK and in Spain who has helped us in the development and the production of these materials. We would also like to thank all the teachers who have taken time to read, pilot and give feedback at every stage of writing the course. Special thanks from Carol to Alan, Jamie and Hannah for their encouragement and support. Special thanks from Mark to Carlos for his patience and understanding.

Acknowledgments
The publishers would like to thank the following teachers:
Ana I. Martín Sierra, CEIP San Sebastián, San Sebastián de los Reyes, Madrid; Ana Mª Muñoz Jacinto, CEIP El Algarrobillo, Valencina de la Concepción, Sevilla; Ángel Martínez Tofé, CEIP Escultor Vicente Ochoa, Logroño, La Rioja; Anna Lorente Clemente, Escola Miquel Martí i Pol, Sant Feliu de Llobregat, Barcelona; Bibiana Comas Planàs, Escola Mallorca, Barcelona; Juana María Torres Medina, CEIP Virgen de Valderrabé, Algete, Madrid; Julia Selma Monedero, CEIP José García Planells, Manises, Valencia; Julie-Ann Eckroth Engelter, CEIP El Tejar, Majadahonda, Madrid; María Ques Jordà, CEIP Son Oliva, Palma de Mallorca, Baleares; Mª Cruz Corrales Fernández, CEIP Santísimo Cristo de la Salud, Hervás, Cáceres; Maripi Arriaga Aznar, CEIP Gerbert d´Orlhac, Sant Cugat del Vallès, Barcelona; Marta Civera Sanfélix, Colegio Sagrado Corazón, Mislata, Valencia; Rafael Aguayo Villamor, Landauri Ikastola, Vitoria-Gasteiz, Álava; Sandra Freire Molina, Colegio La Purísima, Orense; Silvia Cebollada Soriano, CEIP El Tejar, Majadahonda, Madrid; Sylvia Frei Salcedo, CEIP La Cañada, Olías, Málaga.

The authors and publishers would like to thank the following for permission to reproduce their photographs:
Alamy/Arcaid Images pp7(1), 80(tcr), Alamy/Bubbles Photolibrary p82(tr), Alamy/BISP SA p82(tml), Alamy/eurekaimages.com p81(tcml), Alamy RayArt Graphics p76(b), Alamy/Mouse in the House p12(1), Alamy/INSADCO Photography pp51, 82(tcmr), Alamy/Tony Lilley p82(bl), Alamy/MBI pp44(1), 47(2), Alamy/maxstock p81(tcmr), Alamy/Ruslan Kudrin p29(2), 81(tml), Alamy/ Steven May pp56(3), 59(3), Alamy/Picturamic pp44(6), 47(6), Alamy/Radarfoto p81(bcmr), Alamy/ Sandra van der Steen p74(2), Alamy/Shout pp44(5), 47(1), Alamy/ Image Source p78(4), Alamy/Hugh Threlfall p81(bcr), Alamy/V Stock p25(bl), Alamy/ Rob Walls p63(l), Alamy/ David Young-Wolff p47(bm); **Bananastock** pp7(3), 19(l), 80(tl), 26(a), 39(2), 60(a, b), 63(r), 81(bml), 82(tcl); **Brand X** pp80(tr, tcml, tmr), 34(4), 37(4), 76(1, 3); **Corbis** pp39(4), 81(bcl), 82(tl), Corbis/Heide Benser p70(c), Corbis/Steve Cole/Anyone/ amanaimages pp6, 15, 25, 37, 47, 59, 69, Corbis/JGI/Jamie Grill/Blend Images p57(b), Corbis/Rick Gomez p53(l), Getty Images/JGI/Jamie Grill p33(br), Corbis/Corey-Hochachka/Design Pics 45(l), Corbis/Sean Justice p76(5), Corbis/Juice Images p57(a), **Corbis**/Gerolf Kalt p35(a, b, c, d). Corbis/Love Images p38(c), Corbis/Tim Pannell pp56(6), 59(1), Corbis/Steve Prezant p16(b), Corbis/Radius Images pp7(2), 80(tml), Corbis/ul Simcock p81(br), Corbis/Image Source p70(a), Corbis/Purestock/SuperStock p82(br), Corbis/ Leah Warkentin/Design Pics (storytime) pp18, 52, 62, Corbis/Ben Welsh p67(c); **Fotolia**/pressmaster (tl,tm,tr) pp16, 26, 38, 60, 70; **Getty** pp22(1, 2, 6), 15(4), 25(1, 6), (5 cricket, bug,ants), 34(5), 37(6), 39(3), 81(b), Getty Images pp12(4), 78(2), Getty Images/altrendo images p67(a), Getty Images/Mark Edward Atkinson p15(bl), Getty Images/Inti St Clair p59(bl), Getty Images/Chris Close pp34(6), 37(5), Getty Images/EschCollection p82(bcr), Getty Images/Andy Crawford p74(1), Getty Images/Fuse p47(br), Getty Images/sola deo gloria pp66(3, 4), 69(3, 4), Getty Images/Steve Gorton pp29(4), 81(tml), Getty Images/Adrian Green p57(e),Getty Images/Jeff Greenough p41(r), Getty Images/HakanDahstrom p81(bmr), Getty Images/Tim Hall p48(b), Getty Images/Nicole Hill pp82(bcml), Getty Images/JGI p47(bl), Getty Images/Huw Jones p76(4), Getty Images/Jupiterimages p59(bm), Getty Images/KidStock p23(br), Getty Images/Dorling Kindersley p76(2), Getty Images/Dave King pp29(3), 81(tl), Getty Images/Kroeger/Gross p12(2), Getty Images/Margus Muts p74(4), Getty Images/Daly and Newton p78(br), Getty Images/Gary Ombler p74(3), Getty Images/Lori Adamski-Peek p26(c), Getty Images/ Jose Luis Pelaez p53(r), Getty Images/Science Photo Library p82(tcr), Getty Images/Ray Pietro p16(a), Getty Images/Tim Platt pp56(1) 59(4), Getty Images/Susanna Price p78(bl), Getty Images/Floresco Productions p48(a), Getty Images/Image Source p44(3), 47(3), 82(tmr), Getty Images/Image Studios p70(b),Getty Images/Tuan Tran pp66(1), 69(1), Getty Images/Thomas Tolstrup p25(bm), Getty Images/Nicola Tree pp44(4), 47(5), Getty Images/Art Vandalay p38(a), Getty Images/Glow Wellness p55(br), Getty Images/Juliet White p19(r), Getty Images/Christoph Wilhelm pp44(2), 47(4), **Glow Images** pp38(b), 74(bl), 78(1), Glow Images/F1onlineRM p67(b), Glow Images/Julien de Wide pp66(2, 6), Glow Images/Christophe Lehenaff/Photononstop p74(bm); **Imagesource** pp12(5), 15(br), 26(b), 61(1), 82(bcml); **John Foxx Images** pp17, 80(bcml, br); **Jupiter** pp56(4), 59(2); **istock** pp9(l,r), 56(5), 59(5); Macmillan pp22(3, 4) 25(2, 3), Macmillan/Paul Bricknell pp39(1), 56(2), 57(d), 59(6), 81(bcml), Macmillan/David Tolley pp29(1), 81(tcr); **Masterfile** pp66(5), 69(5); **Photodisc** pp7(5),12(6), 17(1, 2, 4, 5, 6,), 15(1, 2, 3, 5), 21(tl), 23(rabbit), 34(1, 3), 37(1, 3),80(tcmr, bmr, bcmr, bml, bl); **Pixtal** pp48(rock, paper, scissors); **Rex Features**/design pics inc pp81(tr), 74(5), 82(bcl); **Science Photo Library** p41(l); **Stockbyte** pp12(3), 22(5), 25(4), 60(c); **SuperStock**/Fancy Collection p59(br), Superstock/Cusp p78(5), SuperStock /Blend Images pp15(bm), 78(3), SuperStock/Design Pics pp34(2), 37(2), SuperStockChevalier Virginie /Oredia Eurl pp48(cards), 57(f), SuperStock/Glow Images p25(br), Superstock/Junirs pp17(1), 80(bcl), Superstock/Kablonk p82(bmr), SuperStock/Science Photo Library p82(tcml).

Stickers
Alamy/Arcaid Images, Alamy/Bubbles Photolibrary, Alamy/BISP SA p82(tml), Alamy/ Ruslan Kudrin, Alamy/Tony Lilley, Alamy/maxstock, Alamy/ Hugh Threlfall, Bananastock, Brand X, Corbis, Corbis/Radius Images, Corbis/ul Simcock, Corbis/Purestock/SuperStock, Getty Images, Getty Images/HakanDahstrom, Getty Images/Steve Gorton, Getty Images/Nicole Hill, Getty Images/Dave King, Getty Images/Science Photo Library, Getty Images/Image Source, John Foxx Images,Macmillan/Paul Bricknell, Macmillan/David Tolley, Photodisc, Rex Features, Rex Features/design pics inc, Superstock/Kablonk.

Commissioned photographs by Stuart Cox pp 6,10,15,16 (tc,bl),21(c,b),26 (tc),31,33(c),35(br),37(bl,bm,br),38(tl),43,45(br),48(tc),55(c),57(br),60(tc),65, 67(br),69(bl,bm),70(tc),75,77,79(br).
Author photograph (Carol Read) by Michael Shelley
Thanks to Mica, Christiana and Harry.

Although we have tried to trace and contact copyright holders before publication, in some cases this has not been possible. If contacted we will be pleased to rectify any errors or omissions at the earliest opportunity.

These materials may contain links for third party websites. We have no control over, and are not responsible for, the contents of such third party websites. Please use care when accessing them.

Printed and bound in Uruguay
2019

How are you, Tiger?

Lesson 1

1 🖍 Find and colour the names.

2 🎧 💬 Listen, repeat and mime.

Hello, Tiger.
How are you?
I'm fine.
Sue
Jay
Tiger
Hello!

play
speak
sing

3 🎵 Listen, point and sing *Let's have fun in English*.

Introduction and review: Hello. Hi. How are you? I'm fine, thank you. play, speak, sing, count, listen, read, write

Lesson 2

4 🎵 ✏️ Listen and write.

5 ✂️ Make the puppets (TB, p159). 💬 Act out the dialogue.

6 🎵 Listen, point and mime. 🎵 Sing *Come to the park*.

Hi, I'm Sue. I'm nine.

I'm Jay. I'm seven.

I'm Li. I'm _____.

Introduction and review: *What's your name? How old are you? I'm (eight). Let's be friends.* climb a tree, eat ice cream, play on a swing, ride a bike, numbers 1–9

Lesson 3

7 Listen and say *The number chant*.
Find and trace the numbers.

8 Find and count. Write the number. Listen and check.

a 20

b

c

d

Review: *How many (bikes)? Where's (number 16)? It's on the (skateboard).* numbers 10–20, *Tiger Tales 1* vocabulary

Lesson 4

9 💬 **Listen, point and say** *The days of the week chant*.
✏️ **Find and circle the classroom objects.**

Monday
Tuesday
Wednesday
Thursday
Friday
Saturday
Sunday

CLASS CHAT

10 ✏️ 💬 **Listen, number and repeat.**
Ask and answer.

a. Can I have a rubber, please? **1**
b.
c.
d.

Review: *Today is (Monday). Can I have a (pencil), please? Here you are. Thank you.* days of the week, classroom objects

1 A Surprise

Lesson 1 Vocabulary

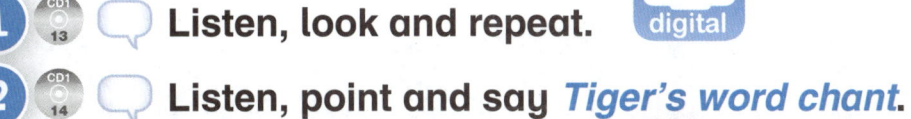

1 🎧 CD1 13 💬 Listen, look and repeat.

2 🎧 CD1 14 💬 Listen, point and say *Tiger's word chant*.

3 💬 Stick and say. Play *Can you remember?*

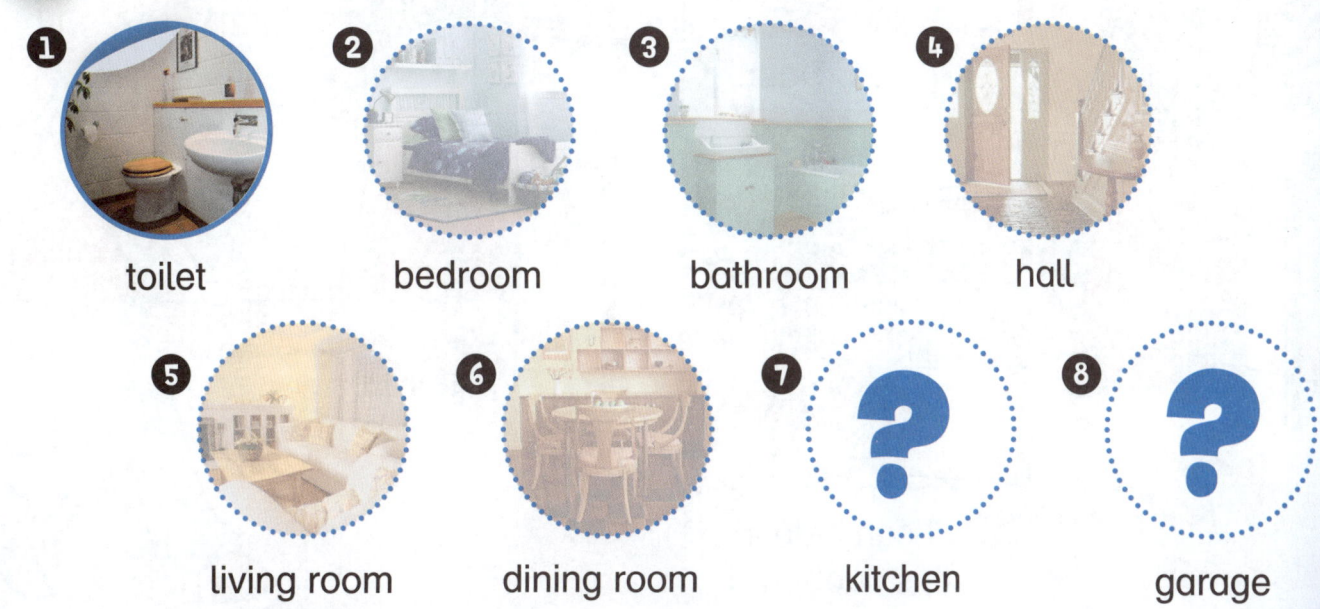

1. toilet
2. bedroom
3. bathroom
4. hall
5. living room
6. dining room
7. kitchen
8. garage

Vocabulary input: toilet, bedroom, bathroom, hall, living room, dining room, kitchen, garage

Lesson 2 Story

4 Listen to the story. Answer the questions. Play *Who says …?*

1 Sue, Jay and Li are in the hall.

… 10, 11, 12, 13 …

2 I can hide in this cupboard.

I can hide next to this plant.

3 Can I play, Sue?

Yes, Tiger.

I can hide in this cupboard.

4 Where's Jay? Is he in the hall?

Story and language input: Where's (Jay)? Is (he) (in) the (hall)? Yes, (he) is./No, (he) isn't. behind, in, next to, under

5 "Where's Li? Is she behind the door?"

"No, she isn't."

6 "Is she under the table?"

7 "I'm in the cupboard. Help!"

8 "Don't be scared, Li. This is Tiger."

Tiger Values

"When you play games, let everyone play."

Personal response and values

Lesson 3 Story activities

5 🎧 💬 Listen and say the missing words.

6 🎧 ✏️ Listen and tick (✔) the rooms Sue looks in.
🎵 Sing **Where's Li?** Look and write.

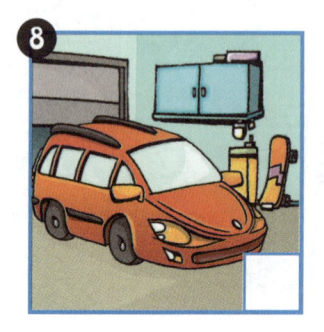

1. hall
2. _____
3. _____
4. _____
5. _____
6. _____
7. _____
8. _____

7 🎧 💬 Listen, look and say who. ✏️ Complete the sentences.

Tiger   Jay   Sue

❶ Tiger is in the _____bathroom_____.

❷ Jay is in the _____.

❸ Sue is in the _____.

Story activities

Lesson 4 Speaking

8 🎧 💬 Listen, look and say.

Tiger Phonics

r**u**bber
c**u**pboard

9 ✂️ Make the cut-out on page 83. 💬 Do a role play.

Is Li in the kitchen?

No, she isn't.

Is Tiger under the pencil case?

Yes, he is.

10 💬 Play *Find Tiger*.

Pronunciation: *The cup and the rubber run under the cupboard.*
Communication: *Is (Li) (in) the (kitchen)? Yes, (she) is./No, (she) isn't. behind, in, next to, on, under*

Things in our homes

Lesson 5 CLIL

11 🔊 CD1 21 💬 Listen, point and say. Read and stick.

1. 2. 3. 4. 5. 6.

| bed | | | | | |

12 🔊 CD1 22 💬 Listen and repeat. Play *Observation*.

PING AND PONG

1.
2. You're dirty. You need a shower.
3. Is the shower in the kitchen?
4.
5. The shower is in the bathroom.
6.

Content input: things in our homes: *bed, fridge, clock, cooker, shower, sofa*

Lesson 6 CLIL

13 🎵 ✏️ 💬 Listen, match and repeat.

14 🎵 Listen and point. 🎵 Sing *The shower is in the bathroom*. Mime and say.

1 **2** **3** **4**

5

Have you got a clock in your bedroom?

15 💬 Play *Draw and ask*.

Content and personalisation: *The (fridge) is in the (kitchen). Have you got a (clock) in your (bedroom)? Yes, I have./No, I haven't.*

Lesson 7 Unit review

16 🎵 ✏️ 💬 Listen, number and repeat. Complete the sentences.

a) She's in the _bathroom_.

b) He's in the _____.

c) He's in the _____.

d) She's in the _____.

e) She's in the _____.

f) He's in the _____.

g) She's in the _____. (1)

h) He's in the _____.

17 ✏️ **Look and write. Complete the sentences.**

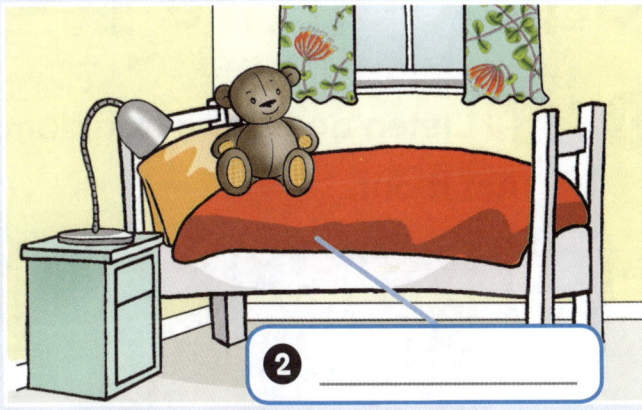

1. sofa
2. _____
3. _____
4. _____
5. _____
6. _____

The _____ is in the living room.
The _____ is in the bedroom.

18 🎧 CD1 26 💬 **Listen, point and repeat. Ask and answer.**

Where's the teacher?

CLASS CHAT

Learning to LEARN ➔ Go to the Picture Dictionary on page 80.

Kids' Culture 1

1 🎵 **Listen and say a traditional rhyme:** *In a dark, dark house.*

💬 **Act it out.**

2 ✏️ **Listen and number.** 🖍️ **Draw and write.**

a. house

b. flat

c. houseboat

I live in a _____.

Intercultural learning: traditional rhyme: *In a dark, dark house*
Language input: *I live in a (flat).*

2 A New Pet

Lesson 1 Vocabulary

1 Listen, look and repeat.

2 Listen, point and say *Tiger's word chant*.

3 Stick and say. Play *Can you remember?*

1. bird
2. hamster
3. turtle
4. kitten
5. rabbit
6. lizard
7. fish
8. puppy

Vocabulary input: bird, hamster, turtle, kitten, rabbit, lizard, fish, puppy

Lesson 2 Story

4 Listen to the story. Answer the questions. Play *Who says …?*

1 Look! Li has got a new pet.

2 What has she got?

3 Has she got a hamster?

4 She hasn't got a lizard.

Story and language input: What has (she) got? Has (she) got a (lizard)? Yes, (she) has./No, (she) hasn't. (She) hasn't got a (rabbit).

5 I think she's got a rock.

6 Help! Tiger has got my new pet.

7 It's a turtle. His name's Tommy.

8 Look! Tommy has got a friend.

Tiger Values

If you've got a pet, look after it.

Personal response and values

Lesson 3 Story activities

5 🎵 💬 Listen and say the missing words.

6 🎵 ✏️ Listen and circle Li's pet. 🎵 Sing *She's got a new pet*.
Look and write.

1. _fish_   2. _____   3. _____   4. _____

5. _____   6. _____   7. _____   8. _____

7 🎵 💬 Listen, look and say who. ✏️ Complete the sentences.

Tiger   Jay   Sue

1. Has Tiger got a ____kitten____? Yes, he has.
2. Has Jay got a _____? Yes, he has.
3. Has Sue got a _____? Yes, she has.

Story activities

Lesson 4 Speaking

8 Listen, look and say.

Tiger Phonics

rabbit
room

9 Make the cut-out on page 85. Do a role play.

Has Li got a rabbit?

No, she hasn't.

Bingo!

10 Play *Sentence bingo*.

Pronunciation: *Ricky rabbit runs round and round the room.*
Communication: *Has (Li) got a (rabbit)? Yes, (she) has./No, (she) hasn't.*

What pets eat

Lesson 5 CLIL

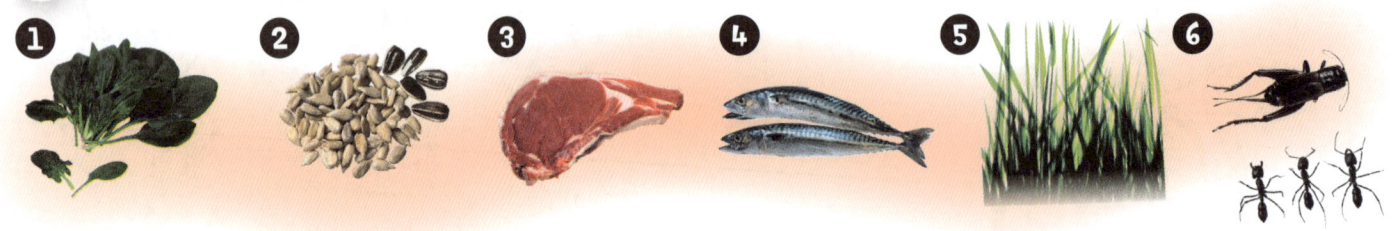

11 🔊 CD1/39 💬 Listen, point and say. Read and stick.

1. 2. 3. 4. 5. 6.

| leaves | | | | | |

12 🔊 CD1/40 💬 Listen and repeat. Play *Observation*.

Ping and Pong

1. Rabbits don't eat meat, Pong.
2. Parrots eat fruit and seeds.
3.
4. Lizards eat leaves and insects.
5.
6.

Content input: what pets eat: *leaves, seeds, meat, fish, grass, insects*

Lesson 6 CLIL

13 Listen, colour and repeat.

14 Listen and point. 🎵 Sing *Different pets, different food*.

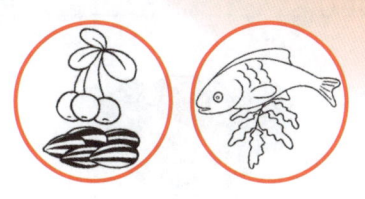

My brother has got a rabbit. Rabbits eat grass.

15 Talk about pets you know.

Content and personalisation: *My (brother) has got a (rabbit). (Rabbits) eat (grass).*

Lesson 7 Unit review

16 🖉 💬 Listen, number and repeat. Complete the sentences.

a He's got a _bird_.

b She's got a _____.

c He's got a _____.

d She's got a _____. `1`

e He's got a _____.

f She's got a _____.

g He's got a _____.

h She's got a _____.

17 ✏ Look and write. Complete the sentences.

1. _____seeds_____
2. _____
3. _____
4. _____
5. _____
6. _____

Dogs eat _____.

Lizards eat leaves and _____.

18 🎧 CD1 44 💬 Listen, point and repeat. Ask and answer.

CLASS CHAT

Has everyone got a pen, a pencil and a book?

Learning to LEARN → Go to the Picture Dictionary on page 80.

Kids' Culture 2

1 🎵 **Listen and say a traditional rhyme:** *Two little dicky birds*.
💬 **Act it out.**

Two little dicky birds …

… sitting on a wall.

PETER   PAUL

2 ✏️ **Listen and number.** 🖍️ **Draw and write.**

COMPARING CULTURES

a. guinea pig
b. dog
c. rabbit

My _____ has got a _____.

Intercultural learning: traditional rhyme: *Two little dicky birds*
Language input: *My (friend) has got a (dog)*.

Tiger Review 1

Everyone, point to the puppy.

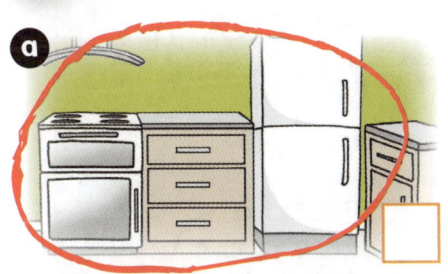

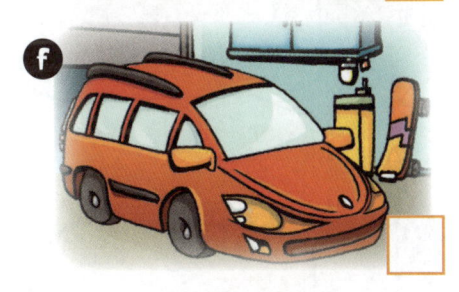

1 Play *Tiger says*.

2 Listen, number and say. Circle red or blue.

a
b
c · 1
d
e
f
g
h
i

3 Draw and play *Guess my word!*

Units 1 and 2 revision

4 ✏️ **Read and match.**
🎧 💬 **Listen and say.**

Can you remember?

1. What has she got? Has she got a kitten? **b**

2. The shower is in the bathroom.

3. Where's Jay? Is he next to the plant?

4. Lizards eat leaves and insects.

a
b
c
d

5 🎧 **Listen and choose.** 🎵 **Sing your favourite song.**

6 🖍️ **Think and colour.**

Units 1 and 2 revision

3 Where's my coat?

Lesson 1 Vocabulary

1 Listen, look and repeat.

2 Listen, point and say *Tiger's word chant*.

3 Stick and say. Play *Can you remember?*

1. shorts
2. shirt
3. coat
4. jumper
5. trousers
6. T-shirt
7. skirt
8. shoes and socks

Vocabulary input: shorts, shirt, coat, jumper, trousers, T-shirt, skirt, shoes and socks

Lesson 2 Story

4 Listen to the story. Answer the questions. Play *Who says …?*

1
It's very cold today.
Look! I'm wearing two T-shirts and a shirt.

2
I like snow, but it's cold.

3
Oh no! Where's my coat?
Where's my jumper?

4
Is this your coat, Sue?
No, it isn't.

Story and language input: *Is this your (coat)? I'm/You're wearing (my coat).*

5 Is this your jumper, Li?

No, it isn't.

6 Look out of the window.

Who's that?

7 Tiger, you're wearing my coat.

And you're wearing my jumper.

8 Tiger! You're wearing my football shorts!

Tiger Values

Always ask before you use other people's things.

Personal response and values

Lesson 3 Story activities

5 💬 Listen and say the missing words.

6 ✏️ Listen and colour the clothes Tiger is wearing.
🎵 Sing *I'm wearing a coat*. ✏️ Look and write.

1. coat
2. _____
3. _____
4. _____
5. _____
6. _____
7. _____
8. _____

7 💬 Listen, look and say who. ✏️ Complete the sentences.

1. Look! I'm wearing a green _skirt_.

   Sue

2. Look! I'm wearing a red _____.

   Jay

3. Look! I'm wearing blue _____ and orange _____.

   Li

Story activities

Lesson 4 Speaking

8 🎧 💬 Listen, look and say.

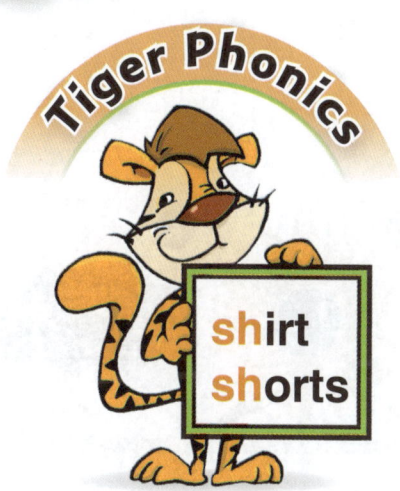

Tiger Phonics

sh**irt**
sh**orts**

9 ✂ Make the cut-out on page 87. 💬 Listen and fold.

"I'm wearing shorts."

"You're wearing a blue shirt."

10 💬 Play *What am I wearing?*

Pronunciation: *Shorts, shoes and a shirt on a shelf.*
Communication: *I'm wearing (shorts). You're wearing (a blue shirt).*

Seasons and nature

Lesson 5 CLIL

11 🔊 CD2 13 💬 Listen, point and say. Read and stick.

1. spring
2.
3.
4.
5.
6.

12 🔊 CD2 14 💬 Listen and repeat. Play *Observation*.

Ping and Pong

1. My favourite season is spring.
2. I like summer, too.
3. I like autumn.
4.
5.
6. My favourite season is winter!

Content input: seasons and nature: *spring, summer, autumn, winter, flower, tree*

Lesson 6 CLIL

13 🎵 CD2 15 ✏️ 💬 Listen, number and repeat.

14 🎵 CD2 16 Listen and point. 🎵 Sing *What's your favourite season?*
✏️ Draw.

a

b

c

d

Your favourite season is winter!

15 💬 Play *Mime and guess!*

Content and personalisation: *In (spring), you can see (flowers) on the tree. (My) favourite season is (winter).*

Lesson 7 Unit review

16 🎧 ✏️ 💬 Listen, number and repeat. Complete the sentences.

a
I'm wearing a _coat_.

b
I'm wearing a _____.

c
I'm wearing a _____.

d [1]
I'm wearing _____ and _____.

e
I'm wearing _____.

f
I'm _____ a _____.

g
I'm _____ a _____.

h
I'm _____ _____.

36

17 ✏️ **Look and write. Complete the sentence.**

1. _spring_
2. _____
3. _____
4. _____

5. _____ 
6. _____

My favourite season is _____.

18 🔊 **Listen, point and repeat. Ask and answer.**

CLASS CHAT

Is this your hat?

Learning to LEARN → Go to the Picture Dictionary on page 81.

Kids' Culture 3

1 Listen and say a traditional rhyme: *I'm a little snowman*. Act it out.

I'm a little snowman.

2 Listen and number. Draw and write.

a. scarf

b. T-shirt

c. jeans

COMPARING CULTURES

In this picture, it's _____.

I'm wearing _____.

Intercultural learning: traditional rhyme: *I'm a little snowman*
Language input: *I like (spring). It's my favourite season. In this picture, it's (winter). I'm wearing (a hat).*

4 Break Time

Lesson 1 Vocabulary

1 🎵 CD2 23 💬 Listen, look and repeat.

2 🎵 CD2 24 💬 Listen, point and say *Tiger's word chant*.

3 💬 Stick and say. Play *Can you remember?*

1. board game
2. hide and seek
3. football
4. basketball
5. cards
6. tag
7. hopscotch
8. computer game

Vocabulary input: board game, hide and seek, football, basketball, cards, tag, hopscotch, computer game

Lesson 2 Story

4 Listen to the story. Answer the questions. Play *Who says …?*

1
- I want to play a computer game.
- Do you want to play cards?

2
- Has everyone got seven cards?

3
- Li, have you got a four?
- No, I haven't.

4
- Sue, have you got a six?
- Yes, I have.

Story and language input: *I want to play (football). Do you want to play (cards)?*

5 I'm the winner.

I want to play again!

6 Tiger! You're cheating.

Sorry, everyone.

7 We don't want to play cards now.

I want to play basketball.

8 I'm sorry, Sue. Do you want to play a board game?

OK, but don't cheat.

Tiger Values

Always play fairly and don't cheat.

Personal response and values

Lesson 3 Story activities

5 🎧 💬 Listen and say the missing words.

6 🎧 ✏️ Listen and circle the game Tiger and the children play.
🎵 Sing *I want to play*. Look and write.

1. *board game*

7 🎧 💬 Listen, look and say who. ✏️ Complete the sentences.

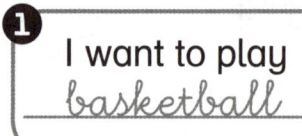

1. I want to play __basketball__.
Jay

2. I want to play a _____.
Anna

3. I want to play _____.
Tom

Story activities

Lesson 4 Speaking

8 🎧 💬 Listen, look and say.

Tiger Phonics

p**ai**nt
g**a**mes

9 ✂️ Make the cut-out on page 89. 💬 Do a role play.

Do you want to play a board game?

No, thanks. I want to play a computer game.

Bingo!

10 💬 Play *Sentence bingo*.

OVER TO YOU

Pronunciation: *It's great to paint and play games at break time.*
Communication: *Do you want to play (a board game)? I want to play (a computer game).*

School rules

Lesson 5 CLIL

11 🎧 💬 Listen, point and say. Read and stick.

1	2	3	4	5	6
classroom					

12 🎧 💬 Listen and repeat. Play *Observation*.

PING AN PONG

1. Can I play in the playground?
   No, you can't. It's raining.

2. (ball scene)

3. (basketball scene)

4. You can't play ball games in the classroom.

5. (table football scene)

6. Goal! I want to play table football.

Content input: school rules: *classroom, gym, corridor, library, canteen, playground*

Lesson 6 CLIL

13 🖉 💬 Listen, number and repeat.

14 Listen and point. 🎵 Sing *In the classroom*.

🖉 Cross (✗) where you can't play ball games.

a b c

d e

f

"At my school, you can play cards in the classroom, but you can't play football."

15 💬 Talk about your school.

Content and personalisation: *You can/can't (play ball games) in the (classroom).*

Lesson 7 Unit review

16 🎧 ✏️ 💬 Listen, number and repeat. Complete the sentences.

a MAX
I want to play _basketball_.

b LUCY
I want to play _____.

c SALLY
I want to play a _____.

d DAN
I want to play _____.

e ALICE
I want to play a _____.

f JOE — 1
I _____ play _____.

g LEO
I _____ play _____.

h LIZ
I _____ play _____.

17 ✏️ **Look and write. Complete the sentences.**

1. canteen
2. _____
3. _____
4. _____
5. _____
6. _____

You can't play ball games in the _____.

You can play ball games in the _____ and the _____.

18 🎧 CD2 36 💬 **Listen, point and repeat. Ask and answer.**

CLASS CHAT

Do you want to sing a song?

Learning to LEARN ➔ **Go to the Picture Dictionary on page 81.**

Kids' Culture 4

1 🎧 CD2 37 💬 **Listen and play the traditional game: *Rock, paper, scissors*.**

rock

paper

scissors

2 🎧 CD2 38 ✏️ **Listen and number.** 🖍️ **Draw and write.**

a computer game

b leapfrog

c cards

COMPARING CULTURES

At break time, I play _____
in the _____.

Intercultural learning: traditional game: *Rock, paper, scissors*
Language input: *At break time, I play (leapfrog) in the (playground).*

48

Tiger Review 2

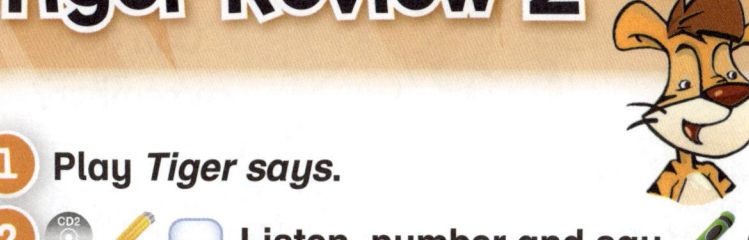

Everyone, point to the T-shirt.

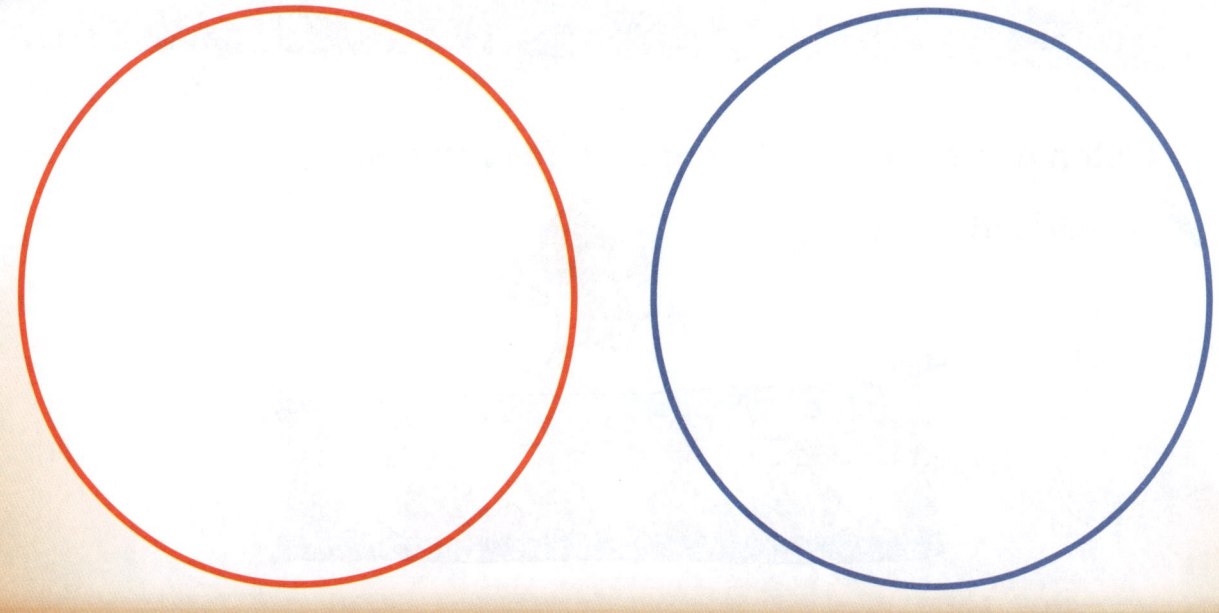

1 Play *Tiger says.*

2 🎵 ✏️ 💬 Listen, number and say. 🖍️ Circle red or blue.

a [T-shirt] 1
b [pile of cards]
c [game console]
d [football]
e [shorts]
f [shoe and sock]
g [skirt]
h [hopscotch]
i [jeans]

3 🖍️ 💬 Draw and play *Guess my word!*

Units 3 and 4 revision

49

4 ✏️ **Read and match.**
🎧 💬 **Listen and say.**

Can you remember?

1. I want to play football. **c**
2. My favourite season is winter.
3. You can't play ball games in the classroom.
4. Tiger, you're wearing my coat!

a
b
c
d

5 🎧 **Listen and choose.** 🎵 **Sing your favourite song.**

6 🖍️ **Think and colour.**

50

Units 3 and 4 revision

5 What's the matter?

Lesson 1 Vocabulary

1 🎧 💬 Listen, look and repeat.

2 🎧 💬 Listen, point and say *Tiger's word chant*.

3 💬 Stick and say. Play *Can you remember?*

1. toothache
2. headache
3. cough
4. cut
5. earache
6. cold
7. tummy ache
8. sore throat

Vocabulary input: *toothache, headache, cough, cut, earache, cold, tummy ache, sore throat*

Lesson 2 Story

4 Listen to the story. Answer the questions.
Play *Who says …?*

STORYTIME

1
- Hello, Jay. What's the matter?
- I'm feeling ill. I've got a headache and a cold.

2
- Hello, Doctor.
- Hello. Come in.

3
- I'm feeling ill. I've got earache.
- What's the matter?
- Please don't cry.

4
- ♪ Don't be scared. Don't be sad. ♪

Story and language input: *What's the matter? I'm feeling (ill). I've got (a headache).*

5 "I'm feeling hot. I've got a sore throat and a cough."

6 🎵 Doctors help us
So we don't feel bad. 🎵

7 "Come on, Tiger."
"Thank you, Doctor."

8 "Thank you, Tiger!"

Tiger Values

When you go to the doctor's, don't be scared.

Personal response and values

Lesson 3 Story activities

5 🎵 💬 Listen and say the missing words.

6 🎵 ✏️ What's the matter with Sue and Jay? Listen and tick (✔).

🎵 Sing *I'm feeling ill*. Look and write.

1. cough
2. 
3. 
4. 
5. 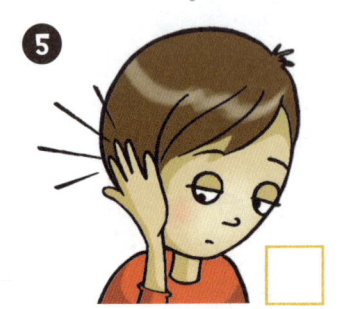
6. 
7. 
8.

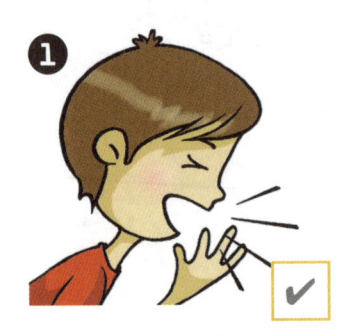

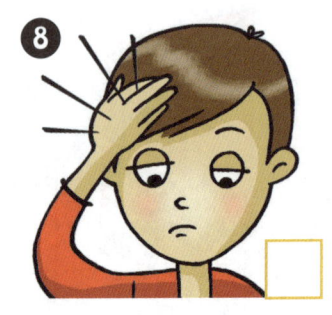

7 🎵 💬 Listen, look and say who. ✏️ Complete the sentences.

1. I'm feeling ill. I've got ___earache___.
   Sophie

2. I'm feeling ill. I've got a _____.
   Tiger

3. I'm feeling ill. I've got _____.
   Tom

Story activities

Lesson 4 Speaking

8 🔊 💬 Listen, look and say.

Tiger Phonics

R**ob**
h**ot**

9 ✂ Make the cut-out on page 91. 💬 Do a role play.

I'm feeling ill.

What's the matter? Have you got a cut?

No, I haven't.

I've got a cold.

10 💬 Play *Have you got a cut?*

Pronunciation: *Rob is feeling hot and he's got a cough.* **Communication:** *I'm feeling ill. What's the matter? Have you got (a cut)? Yes, I have./No, I haven't. I've got (a cold).*

Keeping healthy

Lesson 5 CLIL

11 Listen, point and say. Read and stick.

drink water

12 Listen and repeat. Play *Observation*.

PING AND PONG

1. You need to do exercise.
2. I do exercise every day.
3.
4. I drink water every day.
5.
6. You need to wash.

Content input: keeping healthy: *drink water, wash, do exercise, eat well, play, sleep well*

56

Lesson 6 CLIL

13 🎵 ✏️ 💬 Listen, number and repeat.

14 🎵 Listen and point. 🎵 Sing *Keep healthy*. Mime.

a 
b 
c 
d 
e  1
f

Do you sleep well every day?

15 💬 Play *Mime and ask*.

Content and personalisation: *I (do exercise) every day.*
Do you (sleep well) every day?

Lesson 7 Unit review

16 🎵 ✏️ 💬 Listen, number and repeat. Complete the sentences.

a) I've got a ___cold___.

b) I've got a _____.

c) I've _____ a _____.

d) I've _____ _____.

e) I've _____ a _____.

f) I've _____ a _____. [1]

g) _____ _____.

h) _____ _____.

17 ✏️ Look and write. Complete the sentences.

1. _sleep_ well
2. _____ well
3. _____ exercise
4. _____ water
5. _____ 
6. _____

I _____ well every day.

I _____ _____ every day.

18 🎧 💬 Listen, point and repeat. Ask and answer.

CLASS CHAT

What's the matter?

Learning to LEARN → Go to the Picture Dictionary on page 82.

Kids' Culture 5

1 🎧 CD3 19 **Listen and say the joke.** 💬 **Act it out.**

Doctor, Doctor ...

2 🎧 CD3 20 ✏️ **Listen and number.** 🖍️ **Draw and write.**

a. brush my teeth

b. eat well

c. do exercise

I _____ every day.

Intercultural learning: traditional joke: *Doctor, Doctor ...*
Language input: *I (brush my teeth) every day.*

6 On Holiday

Lesson 1 Vocabulary

1 🎧 CD3 23 💬 Listen, look and repeat.

2 🎧 CD3 24 💬 Listen, point and say *Tiger's word chant*.

3 💬 Stick and say. Play *Can you remember?*

1. beach
2. water park
3. zoo
4. funfair
5. aquarium
6. park
7. ice rink
8. swimming pool

Vocabulary input: *beach, water park, zoo, funfair, aquarium, park, ice rink, swimming pool*

Lesson 2 Story

4 Listen to the story. Answer the questions.
Play *Who says ...?*

1. Look! There's a swimming pool.
There's an ice rink, too. I like ice rinks.

2. Let's go to the beach.
I want to go to the water park.

3. Is there a zoo?
Yes, there is.
Let's go to the zoo. We can see lions and tigers.

4. Oh dear. We all want to go to different places.
I've got an idea.

Story and language input: There's (an ice rink). Is there (an aquarium)? Yes, there is./No, there isn't.

5 It says 'funfair'.

OK. Let's go to the funfair.

6 This is the funfair.

I want to see lions and tigers at the zoo.

7 Look, Tiger. There's a lion.

And there's a tiger.

8 I like the funfair. It's fun.

Tiger Values

When you make decisions, be fair and think about other people.

Personal response and values

Lesson 3 Story activities

5 🔊 CD3 26 💬 Listen and say the missing words.

6 🔊 CD3 27 ✏️ Listen and tick (✓) the place the children go to.
🎵 Sing *In this town*. Look and write.

❶ ____park____

❷ _____

❸ _____

❹ _____

❺ _____

❻ _____

❼ _____

❽ _____

7 🔊 CD3 29 💬 Listen, look and say who. ✏️ Complete the sentences.

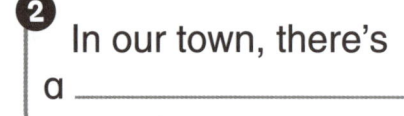

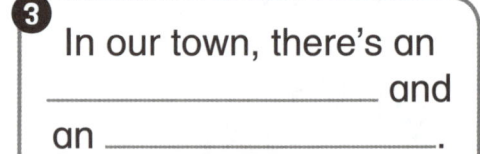

❶ In our town, there's a *park* and a *zoo*.

Sue

❷ In our town, there's a _____.

Jay

❸ In our town, there's an _____ and an _____.

Li

Story activities

Lesson 4 Speaking

8 Listen, look and say.

Tiger Phonics

hair
funfair

9 Make the cut-out on page 93. Do a role play.

Is there a park?

Yes, there is.

There's a funfair.

10 Play *In your town*.

Pronunciation: *There's a bear with pink hair at the funfair.*
Communication: *Is there (a park)? Yes, there is./No, there isn't. There's (a funfair).*

Road safety

Lesson 5 CLIL

11 Listen, point and say. Read and stick.

1. stop
2.
3.
4.
5.
6.

12 Listen and repeat. Play *Observation*.

PING AND PONG

1. Stop!
2.
3.
4. Look left and right, and listen.
5. You can cross the road now.
6.

Content input: road safety: *stop, stand on the pavement, look left, look right, listen, cross the road*

Lesson 6 CLIL

13 🎵 ✏️ 💬 Listen, number and repeat.

14 🎵 Listen and point. 🎵 Sing *The road safety song*.
🖍️ Talk about the signs and colour.

15 💬 Say the road safety rules and mime.

Look left and right.

Content and personalisation: *Don't (stand in the road). stop, stand on the pavement, look left, look right, listen, cross the road*

Lesson 7 Unit review

16 🎵 ✏️ 💬 Listen, number and repeat. Complete the sentences.

a SALLY
Look! There's an _aquarium_.

b JOE — 1
Look! There's a _____.

c LIZ
Look! _____ a _____.

d MAX
Look! _____ an _____.

e ALICE
Look! _____ a _____.

f DAN
Look! _____.

g LUCY
Look! _____.

h LEO
Look! _____.

17 ✏️ Look and write. Complete the sentences.

1. _stop_
2. _____ on the pavement
3. _____ left
4. _____ right
5. _____ 
6. _____ the road

Look right and look _____, and _____.

You can _____ _____ _____ now.

18 🎧 CD3 36 💬 Listen, point and repeat. Ask and answer.

There's a pencil in the cupboard.

CLASS CHAT

Learning to LEARN → Go to the Picture Dictionary on page 82.

Kids' Culture 6

1 🎵 **Listen and say a traditional rhyme: *A sailor goes to sea*.**
💬 **Act it out.**

A sailor goes to sea, sea, sea …

2 ✏️ **Listen and number.** 🖍️ **Draw and write.**

COMPARING CULTURES

a. park
b. cinema
c. swimming pool

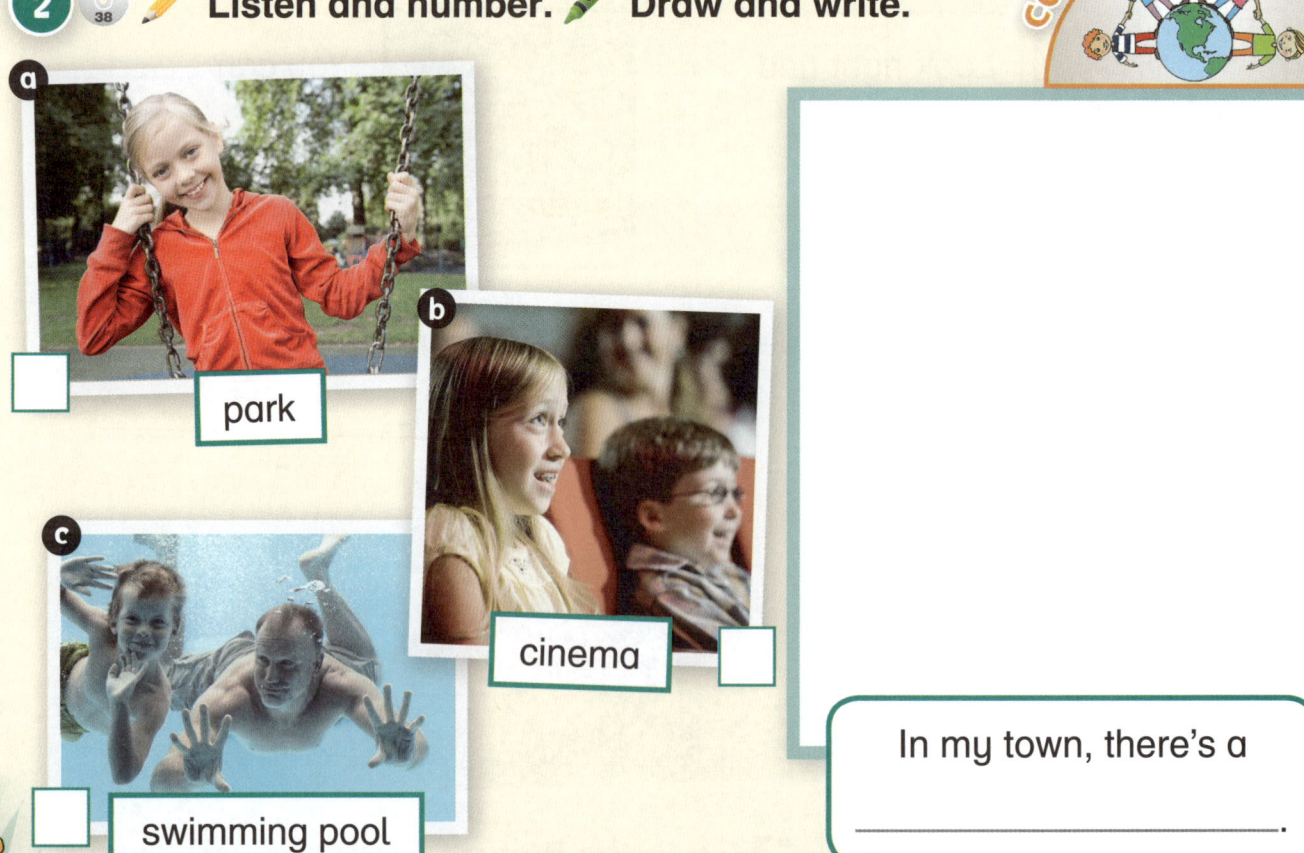

In my town, there's a _____.

Intercultural learning: traditional rhyme: *A sailor goes to sea*
Language input: *In my town, there's a (park)*.

Tiger Review 3

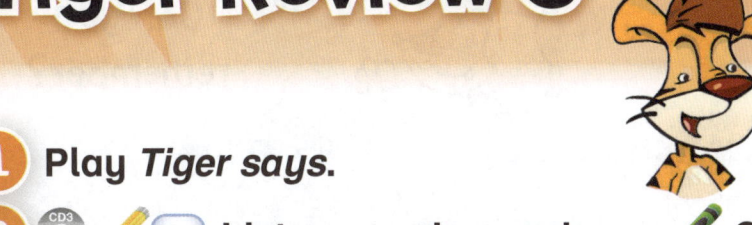

Everyone, point to the beach.

1 Play *Tiger says.*

2 CD3 39 Listen, number and say. Circle red or blue.

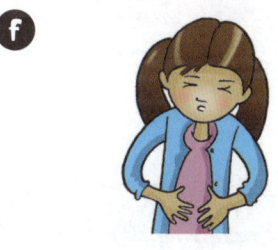

a b c
d e f   10
g h i

3 Draw and play *Guess my word!*

Units 5 and 6 revision

4 ✏️ **Read and match.**
🎧 💬 **Listen and say.**

Can you remember?

1. I drink water every day, Ping. Look! I eat well, too. **c**

2. Stop, Pong! Don't cross the road.

3. Look! There's a swimming pool.

4. I've got a sore throat.

5 🎧 **Listen and choose.** 🎵 **Sing your favourite song.**

6 🖍️ **Think and colour.**

Units 5 and 6 revision

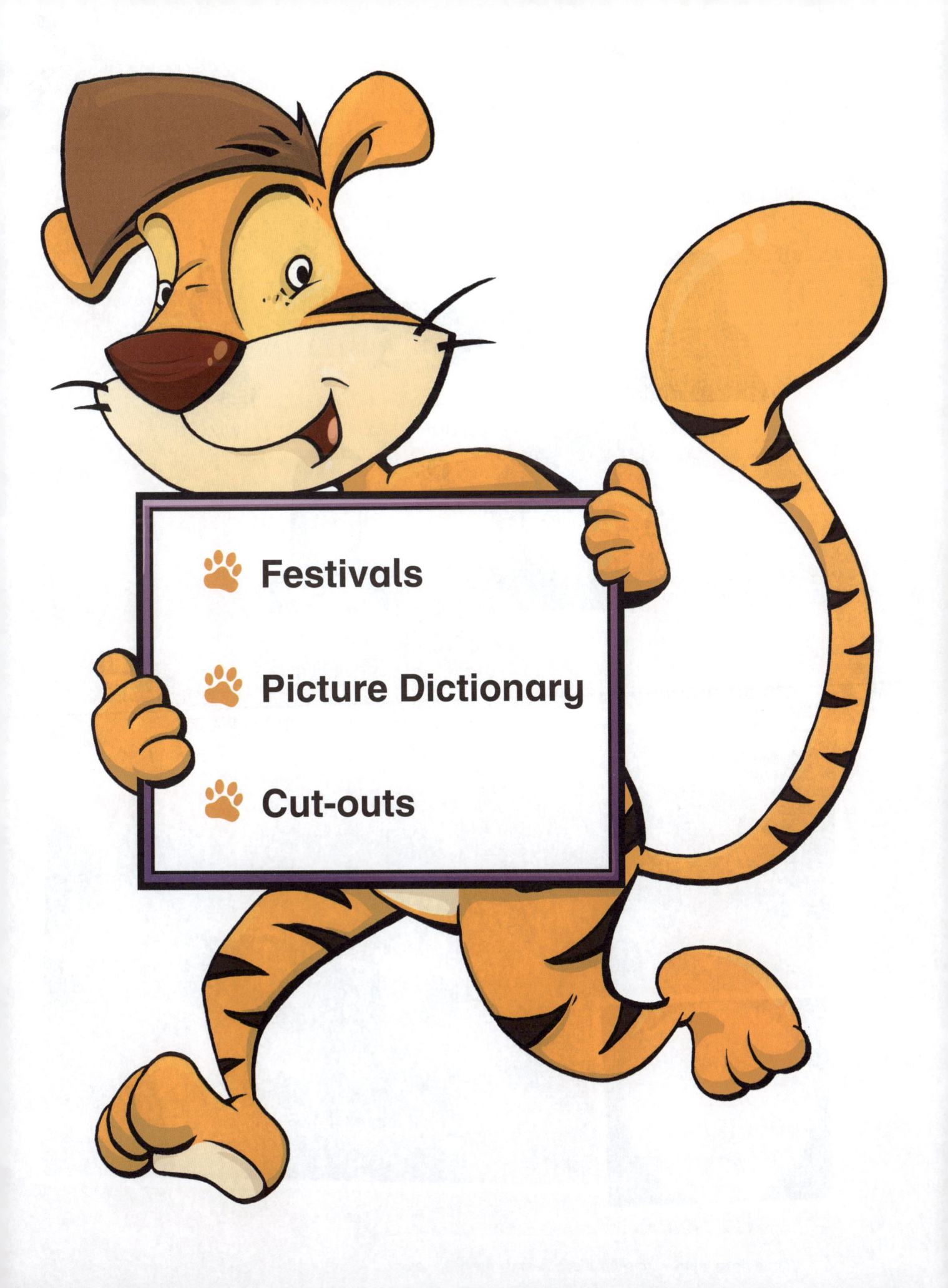

- **Festivals**
- **Picture Dictionary**
- **Cut-outs**

Halloween

1 🎧 Listen and point. 💬 Mime and say.

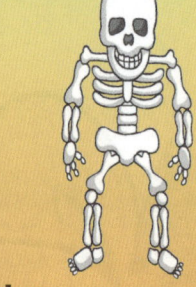

1. monster
2. spider
3. wizard
4. moon
5. skeleton

2 🎧 Listen and find. 🎵 Sing *Halloween night*.

Vocabulary input: monster, spider, wizard, moon, skeleton

3 🎧 Listen and look. 💬 Say *true* or *false*.

4 🎧 ✏️ 💬 Listen, match and repeat.

1 2 3 4

a b c d

I've got a surprise for you.

5 ✂️ Make the Halloween box (TB, p156).
💬 Do a role play.

Communication: *I've got a surprise for you. What is it? Look in the box. It's a (monster). Happy Halloween!*

Christmas

1 🎧 CD4/5 Listen and point. 💬 Mime and say.

1. Father Christmas
2. Christmas card
3. Christmas stocking 
4.  Christmas cake
5. snowflake

2 🎧 CD4/6 Listen and find. 🎵 Sing *Christmas cards everywhere*.

Vocabulary input: Father Christmas, Christmas card, Christmas stocking, Christmas cake, snowflake

3 ✏️ **Look and write. Find and circle.**

1. _ _ _ _ _ _ Christmas
2. Christmas _ _ _ _
3. Christmas _ _ _ _ _ _ _
4. _ _ _ _ _ _ _ _ _
5. Christmas _ _ _ _

S	N	O	W	F	L	A	K	E
T	A	K	Q	Z	V	B	D	P
O	D	C	C	S	D	R	Q	H
C	Y	F	A	T	H	E	R	P
K	I	L	K	B	J	Y	U	M
I	L	Y	E	A	G	J	H	C
N	M	E	B	U	Y	R	W	S
G	V	W	N	J	C	A	R	D

4 🎧 ✏️ 💬 **Listen, match and repeat.**

1 2 3 4

a b c d

Look! I've got a Christmas card.

5 ✂️ **Make the Christmas card (TB, p157).**
💬 **Do a role play.**

Communication: *Look! I've got a Christmas card. What's the picture? It's (Father Christmas). Happy Christmas!*

Carnival

1 Listen and point. Mime and say.

1. king
2. pirate
3. cowboy
4. queen
5. clown

2 Listen and find. 🎵 Sing *It's Carnival time*.

Vocabulary input: *king, pirate, cowboy, queen, clown*

3 🎧 CD4 10 💬 Listen and say. 🖍 Colour the hats.

4 🎧 CD4 11 🖍 💬 Listen, match and repeat.

1   2   3   4

a   b   c   d

"I'm wearing fancy dress. What am I?"

5 ✂️ Make the Carnival mask (TB, p158).
💬 Do a role play.

Communication: *It's Carnival time. I'm wearing fancy dress. What am I? You're a (pirate).*

OVER TO YOU

79

Picture Dictionary

Unit 1

bathroom

Unit 2

bird

Unit 3

coat

Unit 4

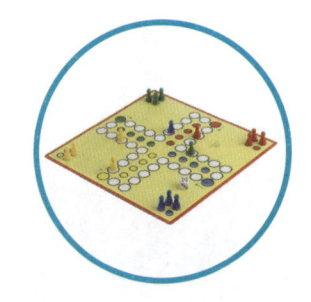

basketball

Unit 5

cold _____ _____ _____

_____ _____ _____ _____

Unit 6

aquarium _____ _____ _____

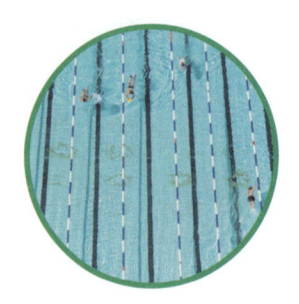

_____ _____ _____ _____

Lesson 4 Make the cut-out. Do a role play.

bathroom

bedroom

dining room

garage

toilet

living room

kitchen

hall

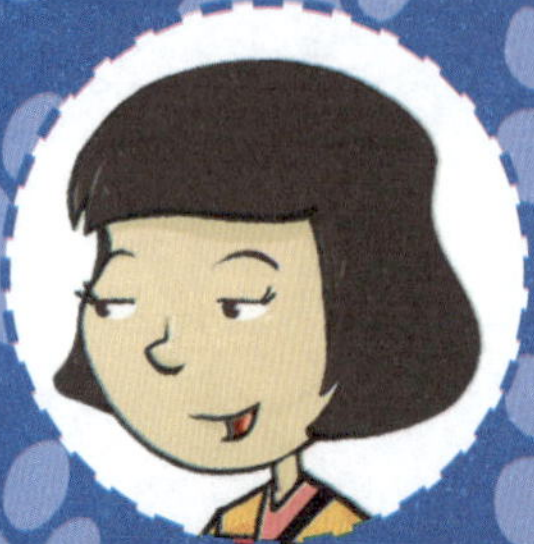

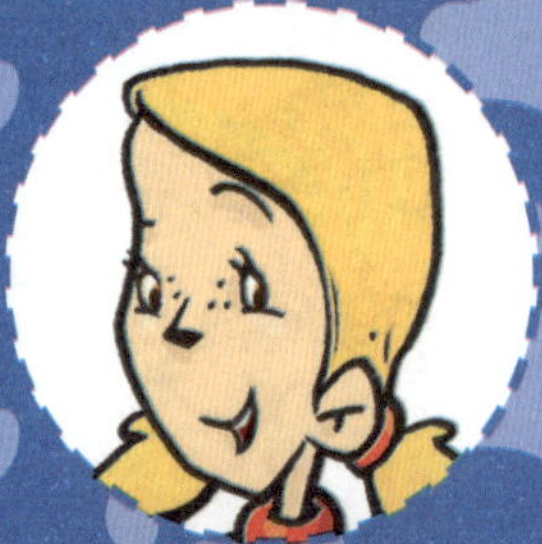

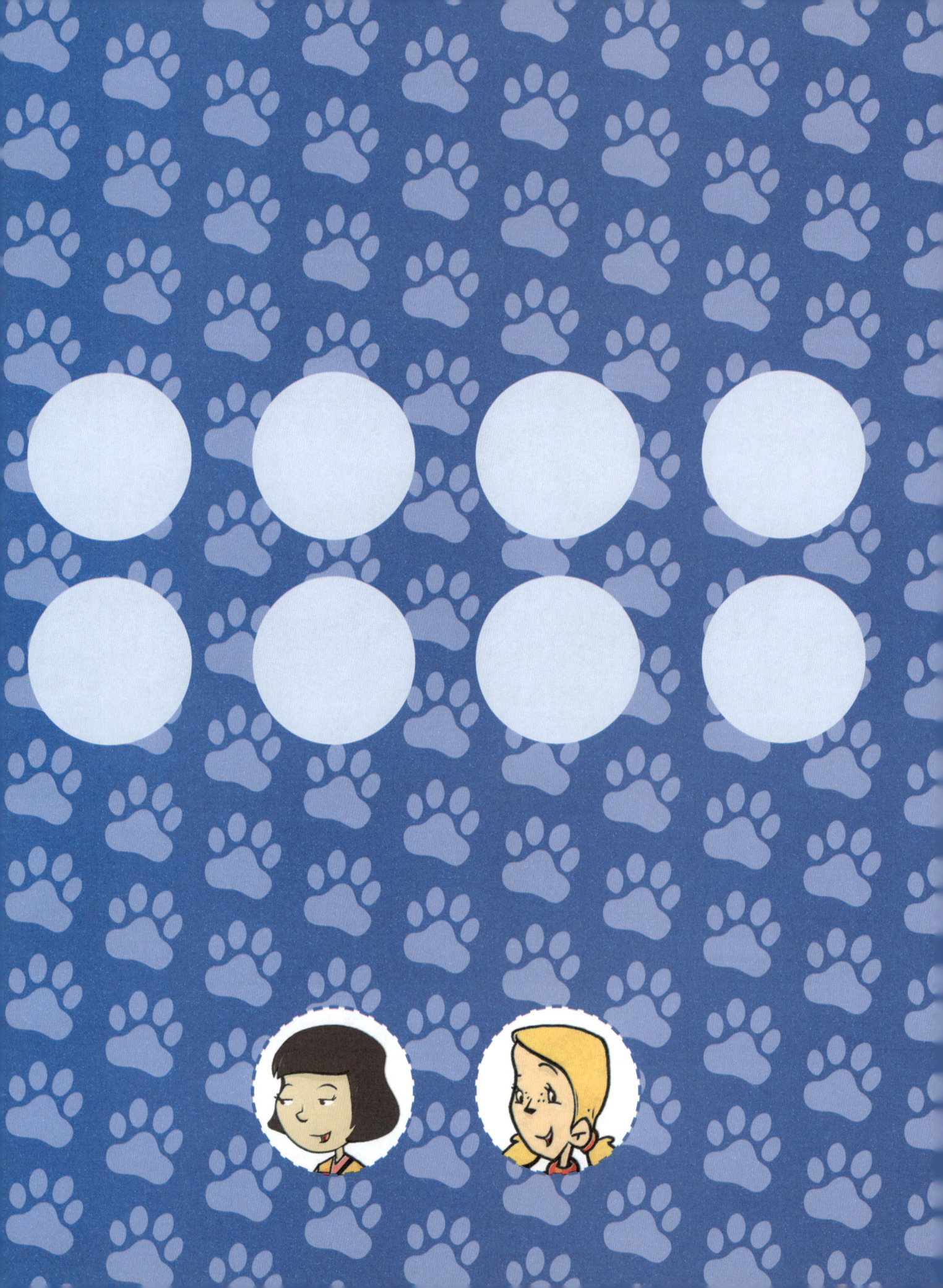

Lesson 4 Make the cut-out. Do a role play.

bird	fish
rabbit	turtle
hamster	puppy
kitten	lizard

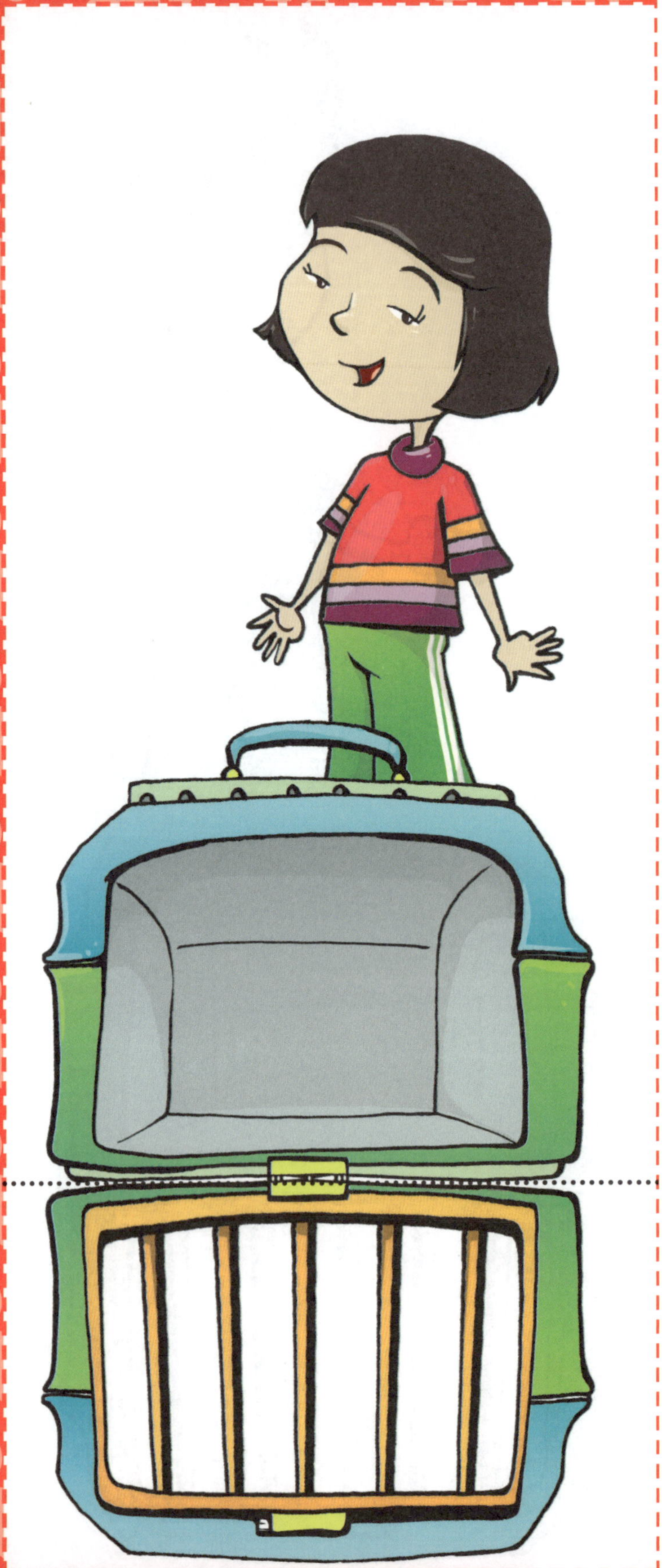

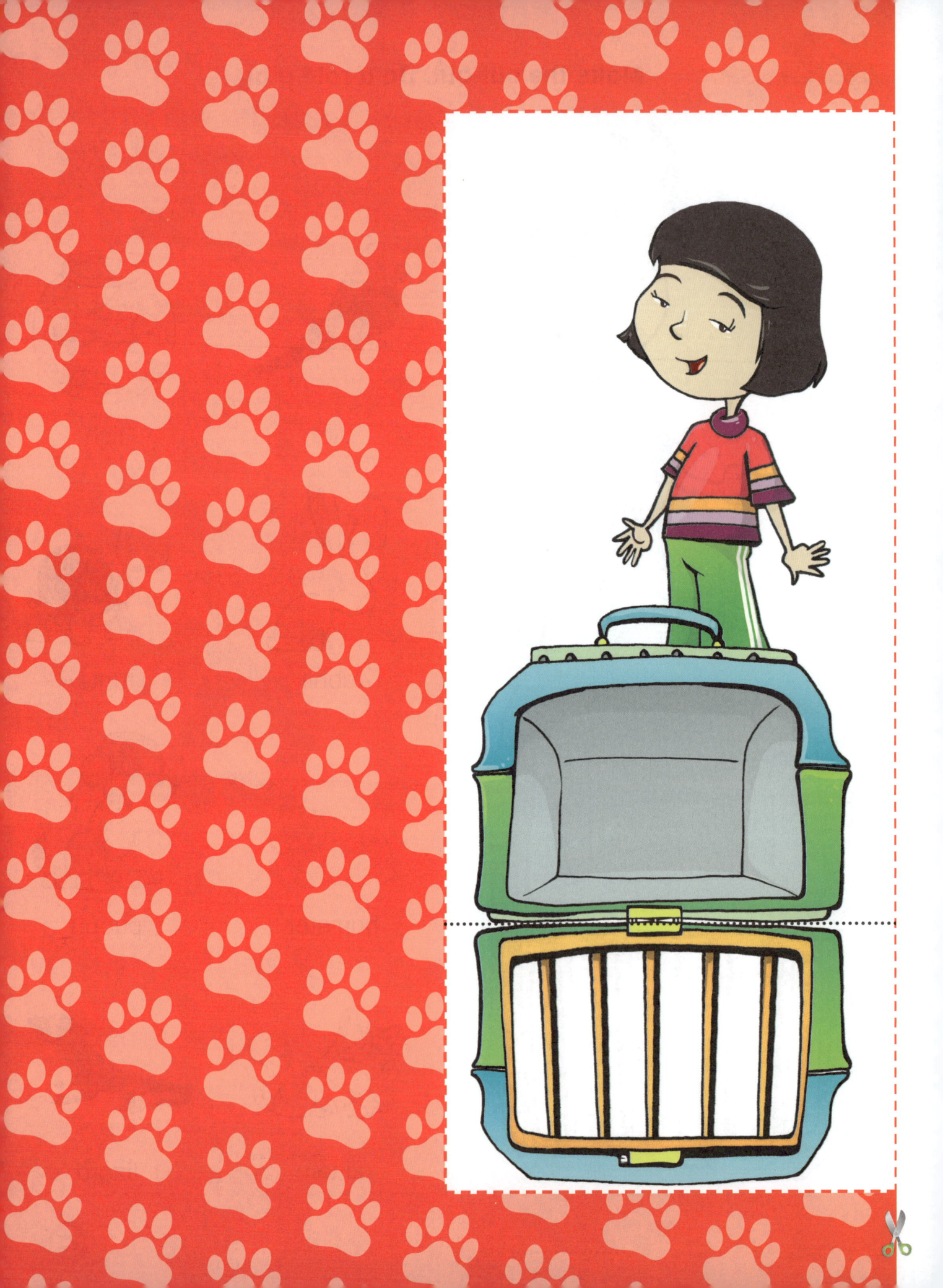

Lesson 4 Make the cut-out. Listen and fold.

hat

jumper

T-shirt

shorts

trousers

shoes

socks

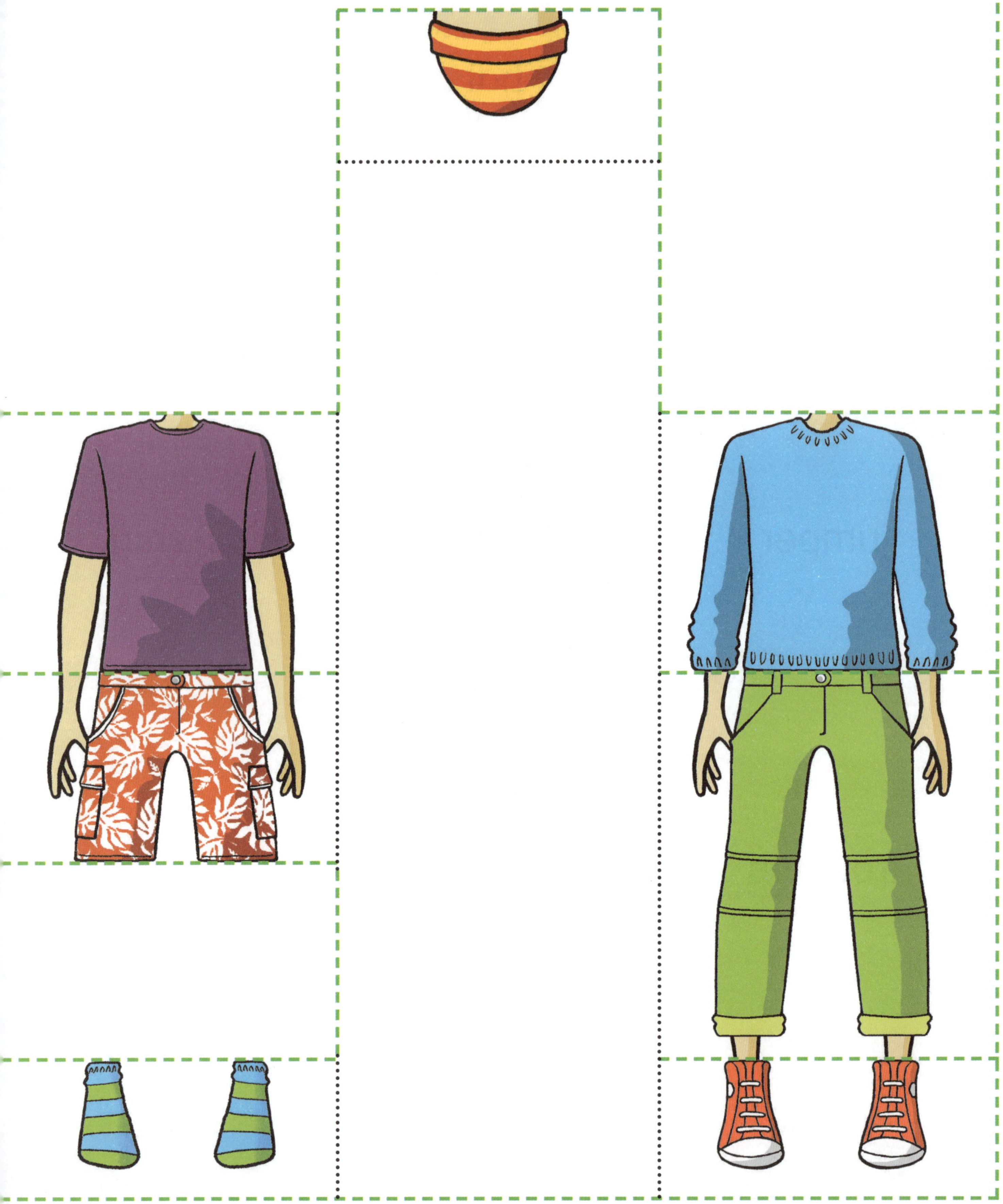

Lesson 4 Make the cards. Do a role play.

board game

hopscotch

cards

computer game

football

... 11, 12, 13 ...

hide and seek

tag

basketball

Lesson 4 Make the cards. Do a role play.

a sore throat

a cold

a headache

a cut

a cough

tummy ache

earache

toothache

Lesson 4 Make the cut-out. Do a role play.

Tiger Tales 2 Syllabus

	Active vocabulary	Active structures	CLIL
How are you, Tiger?	hello, hi play, speak, sing, count, listen, read, write climb a tree, eat ice cream, play on a swing, ride a bike numbers 1–20 days of the week, classroom objects	How are you? I'm fine, thank you. What's your name? How old are you? I'm (eight). Let's be friends. How many (bikes)? Where's (number 16)? It's on the (skateboard). Today is (Monday). Can I have a (pencil), please? Here you are. Thank you.	
1 A Surprise	toilet, bedroom, bathroom, hall, living room, dining room, kitchen, garage behind, in, next to, under bed, fridge, clock, cooker, shower, sofa flat, house, houseboat	Where's (Jay)? Is (he) (in) the (hall)? Yes, (he) is./No, (he) isn't. The (fridge) is in the (kitchen). Have you got a (clock) in your (bedroom)? Yes, I have./No, I haven't. I live in a (flat).	Social Science: Things in our homes
2 A New Pet	bird, hamster, turtle, kitten, rabbit, lizard, fish, puppy leaves, seeds, meat, fish, grass, insects guinea pig	What has (she) got? Has (she) got a (lizard)? Yes, (she) has./No, (she) hasn't. (She) hasn't got a (rabbit). My (brother) has got a (rabbit). (Rabbits) eat (grass).	Natural Science: What pets eat
3 Where's my coat?	shorts, shirt, coat, jumper, trousers, T-shirt, skirt, shoes and socks spring, summer, autumn, winter, flower, tree jeans, scarf	Is this your (coat)? I'm/You're wearing (my coat). In (spring), you can see (flowers) on the tree. (My) favourite season is (winter). I like (spring). It's my favourite season. In this picture, it's (winter). I'm wearing (a hat).	Natural Science: Seasons and nature
4 Break Time	board game, hide and seek, football, basketball, cards, tag, hopscotch, computer game classroom, gym, corridor, library, canteen, playground leapfrog, rock, paper, scissors	I want to play (football). Do you want to play (cards)? You can/can't (play ball games) in the (classroom). At break time, I play (leapfrog) in the (playground).	Social Science: School rules
5 What's the matter?	toothache, headache, cough, cut, earache, cold, tummy ache, sore throat drink water, wash, do exercise, eat well, play, sleep well brush my teeth	What's the matter? I'm feeling (ill). I've got (a headache). Have you got (a cut)? Yes, I have./No, I haven't. I (do exercise) every day. Do you (sleep well) every day?	Social Science: Keeping healthy
6 On Holiday	beach, water park, zoo, funfair, aquarium, park, ice rink, swimming pool stop, stand on the pavement, look left, look right, listen, cross the road cinema	There's (an ice rink). Is there (an aquarium)? Yes, there is./No, there isn't. Don't (stand in the road). In my town, there's a (park).	Social Science: Road safety
Festivals	**Halloween:** monster, spider, wizard, moon, skeleton **Christmas:** Father Christmas, Christmas card, Christmas stocking, Christmas cake, snowflake **Carnival:** king, pirate, cowboy, queen, clown	I've got a surprise for you. What is it? Look in the box. It's (a monster). Happy Halloween! Look! I've got a Christmas card. What's the picture? It's (Father Christmas). Happy Christmas! It's carnival time. I'm wearing fancy dress. What am I? You're a (pirate).	

Unit 1

cooker	sofa
shower	clock

fridge

Unit 2

fish	grass
insects	meat

seeds

Unit 3

winter	flower
summer	autumn

tree

Unit 4

canteen	corridor
playground	library
	gym

Unit 5

do exercise	sleep well
play	eat well
	wash

Unit 6

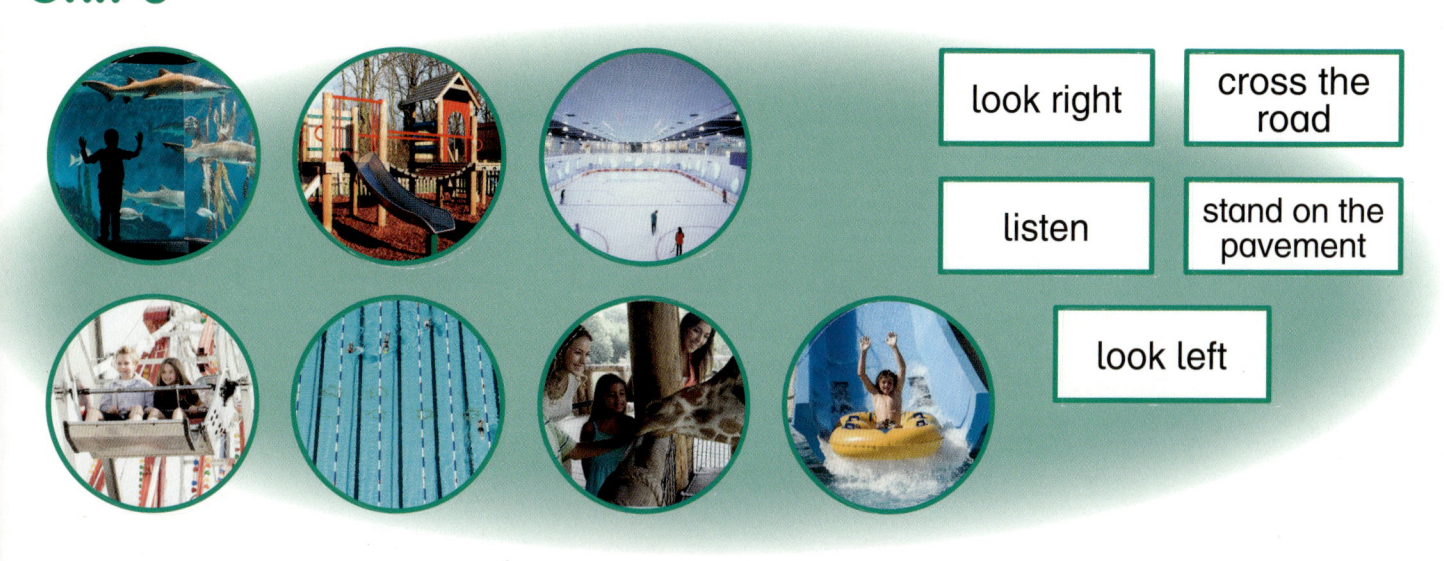

look right	cross the road
listen	stand on the pavement
	look left